**DO NOT REMOVE
CARDS FROM POCKET**

Animal Sounds

Illustrated by Aurelius Battaglia

GOLDEN PRESS • NEW YORK

Western Publishing Company, Inc.
Racine, Wisconsin

ISBN 0-307-62122-7

What does the dog say?
Arf! Arf!

2

What does the cat say?
Meow! Meow!

The little mouse says
squee-e-e-k!

What does the pig say?
Oink! Oink!

The little pigs say
wee, wee, wee!

The cow says
moo-o-o-o-o!

The goose says
honk, honk!

Cock-a-doodle-doo!
says the rooster.

Cluck, cluck!
say the chickens.

The little chicks say
cheep, cheep, cheep!

9

What do the ducks say?
Quack! Quack!
Quack! Quack!

What does the horse say?
Neigh-h-h-h-h!

The flies say
buzz, buzz, buzz!

What do the frogs say?
Croak! Croak!
Croak! Croak!

Buzzzzzzzzzzzzz
say the bees.

What does the crow say?
Caw! Caw!

The little birds say
tweet, tweet, tweet!

The turkey says
gobble, gobble, gobble!

The donkey says
hee-haw, hee-haw!

Baa-baa
　　say the sheep.

Maa-maa
says the goat.

21

What do the owls say?
Whoo-o-o-o-o!

23

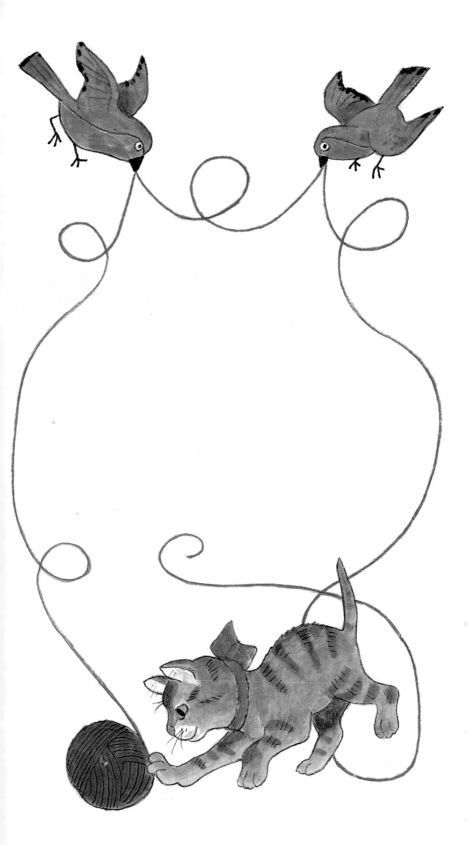